CHARACTER STRENGTH

SELF-CONTROL

Sara Antill

PowerKiDS press.

New York

Published in 2014 by The Rosen Publishing Group, Inc.
29 East 21st Street, New York, NY 10010

Copyright © 2014 by The Rosen Publishing Group, Inc.

First Edition

Editor: Jennifer Way
Book Design: Greg Tucker

Photo Credits: Cover Daniel Laftor/The Agency Collection/Getty Images; p. 4 Bob Levey/Getty Images; p. 5 David W. Hamilton/The Image Bank/Getty Images; p. 6 Darrin Henry/Shutterstock.com; p. 7 Konstantin Yolshin/Shutterstock.com; p. 8 Mel Yates/Digital Vision/Getty Images; p. 9 Rob Marmion/Shutterstock.com; p. 10 Writer Pictures via AP Images; p. 11 Stephen Simpson/Taxi/Getty Images; p. 12 Stockbyte/Getty Images; p. 13 Inti St Clair/Blend Images/Getty Images; p. 14 Image Source/Getty Images; p. 15 C. M. Battey/Hulton Archive/Getty Images; pp. 16–17 Digital Vision/Thinkstock; p. 18 iStockphoto/Thinkstock; p. 19 Rachel Watson/Photodisc/Getty Images; p. 20/Supri Suharjoto/Shutterstock.com; p. 21 DEA/G. Dagli Orti/Getty Images.

Library of Congress Cataloging-in-Publication Data

Antill, Sara.
 Self-control / by Sara Antill. — 1st ed.
    p. cm. — (Character strength)
 Includes index.
 ISBN 978-1-4488-9679-0 (library binding) — ISBN 978-1-4488-9816-9 (pbk.) — ISBN 978-1-4488-9817-6 (6-pack)
 1. Self-control—Juvenile literature. I. Title.
 BF632.A69 2013
 153.8—dc23

                              2012026916

Manufactured in the United States of America

CPSIA Compliance Information: Batch #S13PK2: For Further Information contact Rosen Publishing, New York, New York at 1-800-237-9932

Contents

DISCOVERING CHARACTER STRENGTHS

Imagine two students in class. One is talking to others and does not have her homework ready. The other is sitting quietly and paying attention. His homework is neatly done and ready to turn in. Which of these two students do you think will be more successful in class?

You can probably guess that the second student will do better in school. Like many successful people, he shows **self-control**.

Jeremy Lin (1988-)

Unlike most professional basketball players, Jeremy Lin was not drafted by a team out of high school or offered a college basketball scholarship. He continued to practice, though, and become an even better player. He became an instant star when he played for the New York Knicks. He joined the Houston Rockets in 2012.

It takes self-control to raise your hand and wait to be called on instead of speaking out of turn.

Jeremy Lin showed self-control by studying hard so that he could get into Harvard University. His self-control practicing basketball led to his getting chosen to play for the New York Knicks in the 2011–2012 season.

Self-control means being able to control yourself. You have control over how you **behave**, or act, in different **situations**. Having self-control means that you can make the right choices, even when they are not the easy choices.

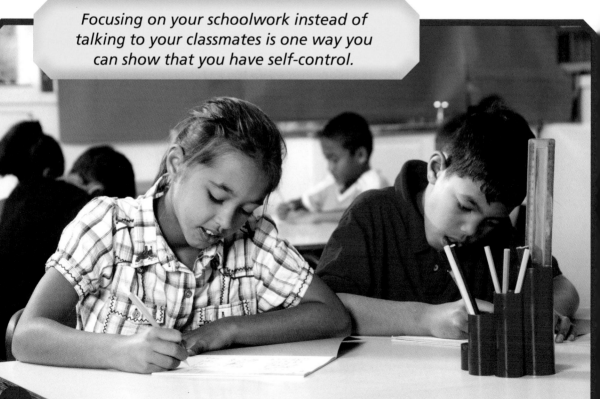

Focusing on your schoolwork instead of talking to your classmates is one way you can show that you have self-control.

Do you keep your homework organized? It takes self-control to take the time to put everything in order.

You can show self-control by being prepared for school, sports practice, or anything else that you do. People with self-control pay attention in class and follow directions. They can resist **distractions** and finish what they start. People with self-control know how to control their **emotions** and are polite to those around them. They are often pleasant people to be around!

YOU ARE IN CONTROL

You may feel that you are often not in control of what you do. You may feel like your parents make you do many things, such as go to school, eat your dinner, and go to bed at a certain time. It is true that kids do not control everything in their lives. What you do control, though, is how you react to each situation.

You need to go to bed earlier on school nights so that it is easier to wake up early the next morning. This takes self-control, but you will likely be happy you did it!

Self-control can help you meet a goal, like saving your money for a special toy.

The next time you feel yourself getting angry or upset, take a moment to pause. Think about what is upsetting you and why. Try to see things from a different **perspective**, or view, before you decide how to act.

BE PREPARED

One of the best places to show your self-control is at school. Like your parents, your teacher controls some of what happens during the day. However, the way you act during the day is up to you!

You can start showing self-control by being prepared for class. It took a lot of self-control for Liz Murray to keep up with her schoolwork because after her mother died, she became homeless at 15.

Liz Murray (1980-)

Liz Murray had a very hard childhood. Both of her parents were drug addicts. She became homeless as a teenager. She could have given up. However, she showed self-control by working hard in school. She even went to Harvard University, one of the best colleges in the country!

Being prepared for school means having your homework and your supplies, such as pencils, notebook paper, and textbooks, ready every morning.

Murray finished high school, college, and started Manifest Living, a company that creates workshops to help people turn their lives around. She wrote a bestselling book, *Breaking Night*, about her experiences.

THE MARSHMALLOW TEST

In the 1960s, Professor Walter Mischel ran an **experiment**. He brought a child into a room with one marshmallow on a plate. He told the child that she could have one marshmallow now or wait 15 minutes and have two. Mischel then tested how long each child could wait without eating the marshmallow.

Being able to wait for a treat is called delaying gratification. This is a kind of patience that requires self-control.

When you delay gratification, you are able to tell yourself that a goal, such as winning a spelling bee, is worth the practice you need to put in.

Years later, Mischel looked at those children again. The children who had waited longer and showed self-control were more successful as adults than the children who could not control themselves. Looking at how much self-control a person shows can help predict, or guess, how successful he will be in his life.

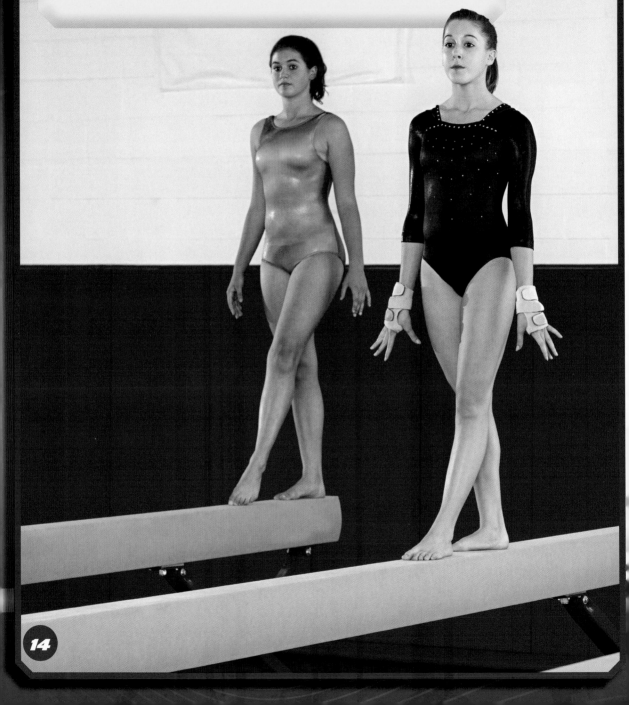

Gymnasts cannot allow themselves to be distracted when they are on the balance beam. Self-control is an inner resource that allows them to focus on this activity.

AN INNER RESOURCE

Can you think of a time when you did not show self-control? How did you feel? You may have felt guilty, sad, or scared of getting in trouble. Self-control is an inner **resource** that helps you make good choices about how you act.

When you are organized, you can **focus** on learning new things. W. E. B. Du Bois was a cofounder of the National Association for the Advancement of Colored People, or NAACP. He was known for being so organized that he often used graph paper to keep track of his busy schedule!

W. E. B. Du Bois (1868-1963)

In addition to cofounding the NAACP, W. E. B. Du Bois was an author and a historian. He was also the first African American to earn a doctorate degree from Harvard University. He was organized, focused, and showed a lot of self-control in his work to fight for the civil rights of African Americans.

ENCOURAGING SELF-CONTROL

The way that people in a group behave can affect how you behave. This is easy to see if you have ever studied with a partner or a group of friends. If people in the group are goofing off, it is harder for everyone to focus. That is why helping others show self-control can help you show your self-control, too!

You can **encourage** your friends and classmates to show self-control every day. If someone is upset, let him know that you understand. Instead of focusing on bad feelings, though, talk about what you can both do to make the situation better.

Waiting in line takes self-control. It is easier to be patient when everyone in the line waits his or her turn, though!

SETTING GOALS

Take a moment to think about how much self-control you show each day. Maybe you are polite much of the time but often fight with your siblings. Perhaps you are a good student but do not always study for tests.

Some goals take years to achieve. These are long-term goals, like graduating from high school or going to college.

It feels good to achieve goals. You can be proud of the achievement as well as the self-control it took you to get there!

Setting **goals** for yourself is a good way to see how you can improve. You might set a goal of studying for 30 minutes for your next spelling test. You can decide ahead of time that the next time your brother comes into your room without asking, you will not yell. When you catch yourself showing self-control, you can feel very proud!

A person with self-control might have free time in the afternoon once he has finished his homework. His sense of curiosity might lead him to sign up for music lessons.

FINDING A BALANCE

We have seen how important self-control is for success. The more you practice showing self-control, the more you will have. There are other character strengths that can help you as well, such as grit, optimism, and gratitude. It is important to find a good **balance** of all these strengths.

People have written about balancing character strengths throughout recorded history. The ancient Greek writer Plato wrote that self-control was one of the four basic character strengths a person needs. He said that self-control helped people strike a balance between wisdom, needs, and emotions.

Plato (c. 424 BC–c. 348 BC)

Plato was a Greek mathematician, writer, and philosopher, or thinker. Plato believed that one of the biggest problems of his day was that people did not have enough self-control. He founded a school in Athens to teach people philosophy so they could be good leaders.

MY REPORT CARD:
SELF-CONTROL

How much self-control do you show each day? On a separate sheet of paper, mark off how many of the following statements sound like you. Be honest about your answers! If you are not happy with your score, do not be upset. Practice showing your self-control for a few days or weeks, and then take the test again.

- ☐ I am polite to those around me.
- ☐ I am not easily distracted.
- ☐ I am always prepared for class.
- ☐ I finish my homework before I start other things.
- ☐ I try to help others solve their problems.
- ☐ I know the way I behave is always a choice.
- ☐ I pay attention to what my teacher is saying.
- ☐ I am good at following directions.
- ☐ I can control my temper when something upsets me.
- ☐ I try to understand other peoples' views.

Glossary

balance (BAL-ens) Having the right mix of things.

behave (bih-HAYV) To act.

distractions (dih-STRAK-shunz) Things that draw one's attention away from other things.

emotions (ih-MOH-shunz) Strong feelings.

encourage (in-KUR-ij) To give hope, cheer, or certainty.

experiment (ik-SPER-uh-ment) A set of actions or steps taken to learn more about something.

focus (FOH-kis) To concentrate.

goals (GOHLZ) Things that a person wants to do or be.

perspective (per-SPEK-tiv) Point of view.

resource (REE-sawrs) A supply, source of energy, or other useful thing.

self-control (self-kun-TROHL) Controlling one's actions or feelings.

situations (sih-choo-AY-shunz) Problems or events.

Index

Websites

Due to the changing nature of Internet links, PowerKids Press has developed an online list of websites related to the subject of this book. This site is updated regularly. Please use this link to access the list: www.powerkidslinks.com/char/self/